D0978875

A Gift For:

_____

The LORD said,
"Surely I will deliver you for a good purpose."
Jeremiah 15:11

From:

_____

Pathway to Purpose™ for Women Personal Journal
Copyright © 2005 by Katie Brazelton
ISBN 0-310-81174-0

All Scripture quotations, unless otherwise noted, are taken from the Holy Bible:
New International Version, (North American Edition)®. Copyright © 1973, 1978,
1984, by International Bible Society. Used by permission of Zondervan. All rights
reserved.

All rights reserved. No part of this publication may be reproduced, stored in a
retrieval system, or transmitted in any form or by any means—electronic,
mechanical, photocopy, recording, or any other—except for brief quotations in
printed reviews, without the prior permission of the publisher.

At Inspirio we love to hear from you—your stories, your feedback, and your prod-
uct ideas. Please send your comments to us by way of e-mail at
icares@zondervan.com or to the address below:

Attn: Inspirio Cares
5300 Patterson Avenue SE
Grand Rapids, MI 49530

If you would like further information
about Inspirio and the products we
create please visit us at:
www.inspiriogifts.com
Thank you and God bless!

Compiler: Molly C. Detweiler
Project Manager: Tom Dean
Design Manager: Val Buick
Design: Michael J. Williams

Printed in the U.S.A.
05 06 07/DCI/ 4 3 2 1

Pathway *to* Purpose™ *for women*

personal journal

inspirio™

Finding our life purpose is rarely easy. For most of us, it is the result of much dedicated—and at times, exhausting—effort. It is not something most of us do well on our own, and I certainly could not have done it without the help of my younger sister, Maureen. She taught me the value of following a proven pathway, complete with mile markers, no matter what the goal.

What I learned from Maureen at first had nothing to do with my search for purpose in life. Maureen had completed twenty-seven marathons and three triathlons, including an Ironman competition in Hawaii. So I asked her to be my exercise coach and help me burn off the lingering flabbiness that was still haunting me from my pregnancies.

During our first training session, she simply instructed me to walk past one house and jog past the next. I began to do so on a regular basis, huffing and complaining, until I could run three entire blocks at a fairly nice clip.

Then Maureen said, "If you can run three blocks, you should try a 5K (3.1 miles) fun race." So I trained hard and crossed the finish line just to show her that I, too, could earn a T-shirt.

Then she challenged me, "If you can run a 5K, you can run a 10K (6.2 miles)." So I logged many more miles with her on practice runs and in races because I enjoyed her company.

I'm sure you can predict what she said next: "If you can run 10Ks, you can run a half-marathon (13.1 miles)."

I eventually ran a half-marathon up hilly terrain in extreme summer heat and won a second-place medal. When the race director announced my name and put the medal around my neck, do you think it mattered to me that only one other woman in my age division had entered the race? No, I had won a medal!

I actually ran an extra mile after that race, trying to catch my sister when she goaded me, "If you can run a half-marathon uphill in the heat, you can run a marathon (26.2 miles)." Believe me, if I had been fast enough to tackle her, I would have made her take it back.

Armed with perspective and a strategic plan, Maureen had been unrelenting about moving me to each new level of competition. Although I soon forgave her, I couldn't forget her most recent challenge.

That marathon and several that followed were highlights of my life. I credit much of the success to my sister, my coach, who clearly understood the process of training for the long haul. Her knowledge regarding each step of the process and her ability to inspire me made it possible for her to pull (and push) me toward the goal.

I find a great similarity between a novice trying to run a marathon and a woman trying to find her life purposes. In both scenarios, you need a guide or partner who understands the entire pathway of where you want to go, one who can prepare you for the challenges and risks that lie ahead. Many women fail to discover and fulfill their significant life purposes because they have no Christian mentor who can instruct them in the proper steps to reach the next mile marker.

If you have a strong desire to eliminate emptiness, fear, boredom, and meaninglessness from your life, let me be your Maureen. Journey with me to discover how each step toward living out God's five purposes for your life will both challenge and exhilarate you. Come with me to where you can get a clear view of the life your heavenly Father has always intended you to live, where your life has significant meaning, your relationships are authentic, and your inner peace is deep.

When you feel that God is nudging you to move forward boldly, breathe deeply and join me on this incomparable adventure along God's *Pathway to Purpose*.

Katie Brazelton
Author, *Pathway to Purpose*™ Series
www.pathwaytopurpose.com

Step Toward the Pathway

Is Your Life Out of Sync?

Do you remember George Bailey, the main character in *It's a Wonderful Life*?
He sinks into a serious depression because of unrealized dreams.
But George comes to understand that there has been a clear purpose in his
life all along. I too experienced a remarkable transformation as I journeyed
on the pathway to purpose. From purposelessness and depression I journeyed with the Lord until he brought me to more meaning in life than I
ever could have imagined.

_____

_____

_____

_____

_____

_____

_____

_____

_____

_____

_____

_____

_____

_____

Can you relate to
George Bailey's
feelings in *It's a
Wonderful Life*? What
are your unrealized
dreams? How have
these made you feel
as though your life
lacked purpose? How
have you been
handling these
feelings?

A Longing for Purpose

At age thirty-five, I unexpectedly found myself divorced. All of a sudden, many of the family responsibilities that for years had defined my life were nearly nonexistent. With no pressing roles to fulfill, I felt enormously dispirited and useless. But in the midst of that purposeless desert, I began an intense spiritual journey through which God slowly revealed to me his multifaceted reasons for my existence.

_____

_____

_____

_____

_____

_____

_____

_____

_____

_____

How are you doing right now in the area of personal validity and life significance?

_____

_____

_____

_____

_____

_____

_____

Perhaps you hunger to do something challenging in your life. Perhaps you began adulthood with great ideas of how you were going to make a difference in the world, but now find yourself struggling to make sense of feelings of emptiness, frustration, or futility. *Dear God, where do I fit? Does anyone really need me? Does my existence even matter in this world?*

_____

_____

_____

_____

_____

_____

_____

_____

_____

_____

_____

_____

_____

_____

_____

_____

_____

_____

> What questions are you asking in your search for purpose right now? Of what feelings are you struggling to make sense?

The whole life of the good Christian is a holy longing.
Saint Augustine, Bishop of Hippo

What do you think about this statement? Have you seen the truth of it played out in your life? How? How might having a "holy longing" lead to a "good Christian" life?

Desperate for Answers

I never expected my journey to begin as it did. My mom gave me a video of the life of Mother Teresa. On the video, Mother Theresa extended an invitation to come to Calcutta. I took her seriously and wrote a brief letter to the Missionaries of Charity in India asking for permission to visit. Then, my mom and I donned backpacks and headed out on a ten-day trip to Calcutta to visit Mother Teresa. That trip would have ripple effects through our lives.

_____

_____

_____

_____

_____

_____

_____

_____

What might be an unexpected first step in your journey? Who or what inspires you in your faith? How could that source of inspiration help you get started in the right direction in finding your own purpose?

Another step in my journey came when I heard a professor speak of Dr. Victor Frankl, a Nazi concentration camp survivor. Frankl gave verbal "injections" of purpose to fellow prisoners on the verge of dying from hopelessness. Sometimes Frankl helped them hang on for the purpose of finishing a painting when they got home or hugging a loved one. I listened intently as my professor explained the vital role of purpose in the human heart. My longing for significance finally began to make sense to me. My search for purpose was a God-designed phenomenon.

_____

_____

_____

_____

How do you feel to know that the need for purpose is a "God-designed phenomenon"? How does this help you understand your longings and desires more fully?

_____

_____

_____

_____

_____

_____

_____

_____

_____

_____

Life Steps Toward Purpose

God designed each one of us to connect with others, to know and become more like Christ, to serve in ministry, magnify him with our lives, and to share the good news of the gospel.

_____

_____

_____

_____

_____

_____

_____

_____

_____

_____

_____

_____

_____

_____

_____

_____

> How do you feel about each of these five purposes for your life? Write about what they mean to your life specifically and how living for these purposes could change your perspective on life.

_____

_____

Can we let go of our well-worn paths and follow the one less traveled? ...
Discovering destiny is far from passive.
Bill Thrall, Bruce McNicol, and Ken McElrath

Leave Your Past Behind

Envision following the pathway to purpose to be like crossing a broad
stream in the mountains. As we anticipate taking our first step, we can
already catch a glimpse of the inviting glades and inspiring vistas on the far
bank. A worthy prize most certainly awaits us! Our urge might be to get
there as quickly as possible, but the stream runs swift and is interspersed
with deep pools. Fortunately, God has provided clearly defined stepping-
stones to help us navigate safely across.

What image comes to
mind as you think about
your journey on the
pathway to purpose?
Are you trying to rush
along the path, or are
you carefully
considering
each step?

Before you take your first step and risk a plunge into the chilling waters, let's pause to make sure you're ready for the journey ahead. Take a moment to ask yourself some tough questions about the pace at which you think you should proceed.

_____

_____

_____

_____

_____

_____

_____

_____

_____

_____

_____

_____

> Can I handle an intense, full-speed-ahead pace right now? Am I physically, emotionally, and spiritually prepared to leave all else behind and strain ahead to fulfill some or all of God's purposes for my life?

_____

_____

_____

_____

_____

_____

The Crucial First Step

The first step we need to take in our search for purpose can be found in Philippians 3:13-14: "Forgetting what is behind and straining toward what is ahead, I press on toward the goal." We need to allow healing to be a legitimate life focus for a period of time. It really is okay to slow your pursuit of purpose in order to concentrate on healing and to put behind you whatever could overwhelm or immobilize you on the journey ahead.

Take a moment to journal about some things for which you need healing right now. What issues or hurts are weighing you down and keeping you from straining ahead toward the purposes God has for you?

The Hazards of Skipping This Step

You may be tempted to skip the step of healing and putting behind. You may consider it to be less important than what God really wants you to do for him. But you could set yourself up for a vicious cycle of unlearned lessons, unsolved issues, and unresolved grief. You won't be psychologically, emotionally, or spiritually equipped to handle any big, new assignments from God if you move ahead too soon.

_____

_____

_____

_____

_____

_____

| What is your first reaction to the idea of slowing your pursuit of purpose to heal and put your past behind you? Does it seem like a waste of time? What might change in your life if you really took time to find healing and restoration before you moved ahead?

_____

_____

_____

No Matter How Dark the Past, You Can Press On

Many women have braved the agony of life, and they know how God can use terrible experiences to bring good out of bad. He specializes in hope, second chances, and resurrections. He's present with you right now, equipping you and nudging you to prepare yourself to do his work on earth. May you find comfort in knowing that if God can find ways to use other women's pain to accomplish his purposes, he can use yours, too.

> How have you seen God use pain for his good purposes in your life or in the life of someone else? How might he be working right now in the midst of the annoying, chronic, unexpected, sinful, or unspeakable struggles in your life?

Your past and present, not only the bad things that have happened to you, but also the good things-your successes, relationships, hopes, longings, morals, motives, spiritual beliefs, self-esteem, and personality-have shaped who you are today. God has chosen to use every part of you in his plan: your mind, body, and soul, your past and your present.

_____

_____

_____

_____

_____

_____

_____

Write down some ways in which God has used, in his plan so far, the aspects of who you are described above. What are your thoughts about the fact that God uses everything in your life for his plan, even the bad things?

_____

_____

_____

_____

_____

_____

_____

_____

_____

The Sojourner's Guide to "Unpacking" the Past

The following suggestions are designed to help you put the past behind and press on toward discovering God's purposes for your life. Take whatever time you need to complete each step.

1. Write about your pain.

   Ask for God's guidance and write down the negative elements of your past, especially the most painful memories you have. Tell God that you want to let go of the concerns of your past, that you want him to take those experiences from you and help you forget them. Forgive others or seek forgiveness. Choose a wise confidante such as a pastor, church leader, counselor, or mature friend to help you move toward healing.

_____

_____

_____

_____

_____

_____

_____

_____

_____

_____

_____

_____

_____

_____

_____

2. Recall a time you healed.

   Write about an emotional or physical hurt from which you have already healed. Now, repeat the same exercise with some emotional hurt you would like to see healed. Envision the challenge you face, then imagine the victory God will give you. God has helped you survive and grow in the past. Let him help you again.

   _____

   _____

   _____

   _____

   _____

   _____

   _____

   _____

3. Prayerfully decide to trust God.

   Decide today to trust that God has a plan to use your past for good. Write a short prayer of decision and commitment.

   _____

   _____

   _____

   _____

   _____

   _____

   _____

   _____

4. Write Your testimony.

Write your testimony in three pages. Try writing one page describing what happened in your life before you knew Christ or matured in your faith.

_____

_____

_____

_____

_____

_____

_____

_____

_____

_____

_____

_____

_____

_____

_____

_____

_____

_____

_____

_____

_____

_____

Now, write one page describing God's mercy and how he has healed you.

Finally, write a final page about your insights on God's purposes for your life right now. Then remember that a testimony is a public declaration. Share it with someone!

_____

_____

_____

_____

_____

_____

_____

_____

_____

_____

_____

_____

_____

_____

_____

_____

_____

_____

_____

_____

_____

_____

5. Ask: To whom will my hurt give hope?

    Identify the type of person for whom you have great empathy, one who might benefit from hearing about your hardships and hope. Write a short prayer here, asking for God's leading and opportunities to share your journey with someone who might need encouragement.

    _____

    _____

    _____

    _____

    _____

    _____

    _____

    _____

6. Surround yourself with people of hope.

    List some people whom you would like to seek out for mentoring and prayer as you begin the pathway to purpose. Write a prayer, asking God to lead you to people who can help guide you along your journey.

    _____

    _____

    _____

    _____

    _____

    _____

    _____

Personal Pathway Questions

1. List five things that have caused you grief, pain, hurt, rejection, or failure (i.e., cancer, sexual abuse, bankruptcy, adultery, infertility, miscarriage, abortion, death of a loved one, unemployment, theft, prejudice, natural disaster, etc.).

   1. _____

   2. _____

   3. _____

   4. _____

   5. _____

2. How has God used one or more of these things for good in your life?

   _____

   _____

   _____

   _____

   _____

   _____

   _____

   _____

   _____

   _____

   _____

3. God can also use your successes or happy memories in his plan for your life. Go ahead and list five such things (i.e., teaching a new believer about Christ, saving money for your kids' college education, healing a broken relationship, nurturing a solid marriage, raising moral children, completing a race, overcoming an addiction, getting a bonus, buying a home, seeing the world, etc.).

   1. _____

   2. _____

   3. _____

   4. _____

   5. _____

4. How has God used one or more of these things for good in your life?

   _____

   _____

   _____

   _____

   _____

   _____

   _____

   _____

   _____

   _____

   _____

5. How could a combination of things on your lists be used to give hope to someone else?

_____

_____

_____

_____

_____

_____

_____

_____

_____

_____

_____

_____

_____

_____

_____

_____

_____

_____

_____

_____

God's Wisdom for the Pathway

The "Mary Magdalene" Step of Life:
Forget What Is Behind and Press On Toward the Goal.

For a lesson from Mary Magdalene, a repentant sinner, read Luke 8:2 and John 20:1-18. Her story of God's mercy has been told for centuries as an encouragement to billions around the world.

Will you let God use your life of pain, grief, problems, failure, and forgiven sin? Are you willing to let your past demons, delays, distrust, and destroyed dreams give hope to someone else?

Never Walk Alone

Do What Matters *Today*

I know it is rather plain looking and not very inviting, but the stepping-stone of *learning to do today what God sent you into the world to do* is firmly embedded in the stream. I know that the mundane responsibilities of today may seem impossibly far away from the glorious purpose you long for. But there is a strong connection between going *today* where you have been sent *today* and a future, take-your-breath-away assignment from God.

_____

_____

_____

_____

_____

_____

_____

_____

_____

_____

_____

List some of the mundane responsibilities you face each day. Write down some ideas of how these everyday tasks might be preparing you for a larger purpose in the future.

_____

_____

God Values Today

You were born to make a Christlike difference in hundreds of ordinary ways, not to ignore or avoid the present opportunities while looking for a bigger, more noticeable project. Despite the relentless tedium of life's ordinary tasks, there are wonderful blessings to be found in doing today what God has sent you into the world to do. Once we begin to appreciate the treasure of today's roles, we begin to experience the stress-reducing benefits of peace and rest.

What wonderful blessings have you received in the past when you did an ordinary task with the love of Jesus? How can you make a Christlike difference today at work, home, school, or wherever it is you find yourself?

So, What About *Your* Roles?

Do you realize that each role you play in your life makes you a valuable missionary for Christ? Your work as God's missionary takes place in your home, church, office, school, neighborhood, state, or nation. Your assignment, done through the love of Jesus in conjunction with and for the benefit of others, touches any immediate circumstances in which you are involved.

_____

_____

_____

_____

_____

_____

_____

_____

_____

_____

What roles do you play in your life right now (mother, wife, employee, Sunday school teacher, etc.)? How would you evaluate the "missionary status" of your current roles? How can you show the love of Jesus in those roles today?

Years Later, the Puzzle Pieces Fit Together

I believe that even in the midst of your ordinary routine, God reveals hints about what he's called you to do. Your daily roles are incredible opportunities for you to use your natural and spiritual giftedness to help your family, friends, and neighbors learn about and become more like Christ. God breathed those traits into you purposefully to help you share his message in your everyday world.

_____

_____

_____

_____

_____

_____

_____

_____

_____

_____

_____

_____

> What in your ordinary routine might be a hint to you about your calling from God? What natural gifts and talents show up in your everyday life? Ask God to open your eyes to these clues about your ultimate purpose.

_____

_____

_____

_____

The Sojourner's Guide to Doing What Matters Today

The following suggestions are designed to help you begin fulfilling your purposes for today so that you can press on toward discovering God's ultimate purpose for your life. Take whatever time you need to complete each step.

1. Prioritize your roles.

   It's hard to find purpose if we're unclear about our priorities. So take the time to consider your most important roles and prioritize them in your mind, heart, and schedule. Make a commitment today to live by this list as much as possible:

   a. What is my most important role in life? _____

   b. Second most important role in life? _____

   c. Third most important role in life? _____

   d. Fourth most important role in life?_____

   e. Fifth most important role in life?_____

2. Take good care of yourself.

   If you are going to go the distance for God, you must take care of the physical temple in which you live.

   Ask yourself: "Am I exercising, eating right, getting enough rest, drinking enough water, and enjoying laughter breaks?" If not, what three things would you like to do to improve your self-care during the next 30 days?

   _____

   _____

   _____

   _____

   _____

3. Don't panic.

   Life is not fair. We live in a fallen world. Tough times are inevitable. So, don't panic! God's highest purposes can be extremely difficult or utterly exhausting for a time. No matter what roles you fulfill or challenges you face, please realize that God will not abandon you.

   What is the role or task that presses your panic button? How can you depend on God to be your strength in that situation?

   _____

   _____

   _____

   _____

4. Prayerfully decide to trust God.

   Write a prayer of decision and ask for God's help to trust him more.

   _____

   _____

   _____

   _____

5. Seize the moment.

   Don't miss the daily parade of life by looking for the circus tent and magic show! What "parades" do you tend to miss? Think of what you can do to seize the moments all around you.

   _____

   _____

   _____

   _____

Personal Pathway Questions

1. You fill many roles in your sphere of influence. Write a brief,
    creative description of who you are in some of those roles. Here
    are a few to illustrate how diverse your roles may be:

    Family Financial Manager
    Logistician
    Television Cop
    Keeper of Family Heritage and Traditions
    Chief Cook and Bottle Washer

    Who Am I?

    _____

    _____

    _____

    _____

    _____

    _____

    _____

    _____

2. In what ways are you surprised or impressed at how many roles
    you're trying to fill?

    _____

    _____

    _____

    _____

    _____

God's Wisdom for the Pathway

The "Lydia" Step of Life:
Do Today What God Sent You Into the World to Do.

For a lesson about how to embrace your current roles in life, read Acts 16:11-15, 40. Lydia was a successful businesswoman who was widely known in cities near and far for selling dyed purple cloth and dyed goods to many households, including those of royalty. In addition, she was a worshipper of God. After she heard Paul preach, she was baptized and became the first convert to Christianity in all of Europe! Lydia then opened her home to Paul and the other disciples of Jesus.

_____

_____

_____

_____

_____

_____

_____

_____

_____

_____

_____

_____

_____

> Are you, like Lydia, embracing your everyday assignments in life, whether that is as a household engineer, career woman, ministry leader, or other vital role?

Love Others as Jesus Loves You

You may find the next stepping-stone on the pathway to purpose to be much more inviting than the previous one. This ancient, well-worn stone is *love each other as Jesus loves you.* Take whatever time you need to ensure that this important step connects permanently in your heart and mind. Loving as Jesus loves is one of your most basic life purposes. It is critical to every life purpose God has in mind for you.

_____

_____

_____

_____

_____

_____

_____

_____

_____

_____

_____

_____

_____

> Why is loving as Jesus loves "critical to every life purpose"? How would you evaluate yourself on how much you love others? How would you like to improve in this area?

_____

_____

_____

The Lesson We Never Stop Learning

Jesus summed up the essence of love when he said, "My command is this: Love each other as I have loved you. Greater love has no one than this, that he lay down his life for his friends" (John 15:12-13). We must never forget that becoming a woman who loves others as Jesus loves is not merely a pleasant suggestion, it is a biblical mandate. Love is the proof of our commitment to Christ. Loving others will always be a growth step for us. No matter how healthy or loving our relationships already are, Christ's exemplary love can always teach us more.

_____

_____

_____

_____

_____

_____

_____

_____

_____

> Why is love proof of our commitment to Christ? How does it show others that we love Jesus when we love them? In what ways can you apply the example of Christ's love in your current relationships?

_____

_____

_____

_____

When we focus on loving as Jesus loves, an amazing cycle is set in motion. First, our love for him grows. Our increasing love leads us to worship, which further deepens our relationship with him. Then, as we establish healthy, warmhearted relationships with others, our lives become a bridge to Jesus for those we love. In turn, our relationships with others become a support for us during times of discouragement and a delight during times of celebration.

Where are you currently in this cycle of love? What is the next step you need to take? What can you do today to grow in your love for Jesus and for others?

The Sojourner's Guide to Loving Others

If your desire is to grow in the love of Jesus and express that love through your relationships with others, then you're ready to press on toward God's next purpose for your life. Take time out to consider and follow through on the suggestions below. They will help you develop your relationships and nurture your love for others and for God.

1. Catch yourself making a loving difference.

   For one week, make a note of anything you do that makes a loving difference in someone's life. This exercise will raise your awareness that you are fulfilling one of your life purposes by endeavoring to love God's people. Start looking for daily opportunities to love others.

Monday: _____

_____

Tuesday: _____

_____

Wednesday: _____

_____

Thursday: _____

_____

Friday:_____

_____

Saturday: _____

_____

Sunday:_____

_____

2. Get connected at church.

   If you haven't done so already, become involved in a local church. The depth and longevity of church family friendships may surprise you and bless you for many years to come.

   Write down some programs or groups that you are interested in investigating at your church. Make a plan to check them out in the next week and write down your findings here.

   _____

   _____

   _____

   _____

   _____

   _____

   _____

   _____

   _____

   _____

   _____

   _____

   _____

   _____

   _____

   _____

   _____

   _____

3. Offer forgiveness.

    Forgive someone today. Don't put it off. Simply pray for the right timing and do it. Forgive in honor of Jesus' forgiveness of you. If you need to forgive yourself, the advice is the same: just do it!

    Prayerfully consider whom you need to forgive. Write their names here and make a plan to speak with them, if possible. Record the results once you have taken this step of faith.

4. Take a relational opportunities checkup.

   What specific relational habits, such as those listed here, do you need to develop right now?

   • If you have lost a job, have you considered joining a business networking group?

   • If your spouse has died some time ago, is now the time to begin building new relationships through outings, socializing, or dating?

   • If you have you been working on building a strong marriage, have you been bonding and communicating with your husband by going on regularly scheduled dates?

   • If you have had a miscarriage, have you considered letting others in a similar situation help you by joining a support group?

   • If you have been attempting to kick an addiction—whether it be to cigarettes, gambling, pornography, sex, alcohol, drugs, or food—have you begun your recovery with the help of a support group or clinic?

   • If you need guidance regarding your finances, faith, family, vocation, etc., have you sought out a Christian counselor or mentor who can advise you?

   • If you are trying to discover your purpose in life, have you read *Conversations on Purpose* from this book series and chosen a Purpose Partner to walk with you through those conversations?

   _____

   _____

   _____

   _____

Personal Pathway Questions

1. How successful have you been lately in obeying God's command to "love one another"?

   _____

   _____

2. With whom do you currently have a healthy relationship? This listing of groups may help you think of specific names:

Immediate Family	Extended Family	Church
Clubs/Organizations	Gym	Small Group
Neighbors	Work	Sports
Christian Ministry Friends	Community Volunteers	School
Parents of Children's Friends	Support Group	Other

   List the names:

   _____

   _____

   _____

   _____

   _____

   _____

   _____

   _____

   _____

   _____

   _____

3. With whom do you currently have an unhealthy relationship? (Hint: Just think of those whose company encourages you to avoid God or stimulates sinful thoughts or actions.)

List the first names:

_____

_____

_____

_____

_____

_____

_____

_____

_____

_____

_____

_____

_____

_____

_____

_____

_____

_____

_____

_____

_____

4. Healthy relationships are a prayerful choice. Is cultivating or terminating a particular relationship more critical to your spiritual well-being right now?

    What is God nudging you to do about one or more of your relationships?

    _____

    _____

    _____

    _____

    _____

    _____

    _____

    _____

    _____

    _____

    _____

    _____

    _____

    _____

    _____

    _____

    _____

    _____

    _____

    _____

    _____

    _____

    _____

    _____

    _____

    _____

God's Wisdom for the Pathway
The "Ruth" Step of Life:
Love Each Other as Jesus Loves You.

For a lesson from Ruth, a loving daughter-in-law to Naomi, read Ruth 1-4.
Ruth teaches us about love, loyalty, kindness, and faithfulness.

How strong is your love for your family and extended family? Pray that God will reveal to you one particular relationship in which he would like you to invest more love, time, energy, and/or resources.

Follow in Jesus' Footsteps

God's Purpose for You: To Know Christ and Become Like Him

Pursue Peace

Our next stepping-stone, seek peace and pursue it, may well be the most sought after rock in the entire stream. Women want peace, and they want it badly. Inner peace not only sounds appealing, but it is worth the cost of pursuit, particularly if you have been feeling distracted, unhappy, or dissatisfied with life.

_____

_____

_____

_____

_____

_____

_____

_____

_____

_____

_____

_____

_____

_____

> Did you realize that God commands us to pursue peace (see Psalm 34:14)? What do you think of this command? Have you ever actively pursued inner peace? How do you think this is done?

What Makes Peace So Precious?

First and foremost, peace is most precious because of where we find it. Finding peace has far more to do with sitting in Jesus' presence than it does with doing anything else. Who but our Lord would give us a specific purpose to pursue peace and then arrange it so that our pursuit would lead us to hearing his will in all areas of life? What a stress reliever! Peace is also precious because obeying God's command to seek and pursue peace gives you a bona fide focus for today.

How has the pursuit of peace in your life led to purpose, stress relief, and greater intimacy with Jesus? If you have not experienced these benefits of the pursuit of peace, what might you do, even today, to begin seeking this purpose in your life?

I Simply *Must* Find Peace!

Approximately one year after my trip to India, I decided to schedule a personal, spiritual retreat to Ireland to meet Mairead Corrigan Maguire, the founder of the Peace People. For several days after my arrival I drank in the lush green countryside. Then, one evening Mairead invited me for a chat. She said, "Pray and listen closely to God all day long. Be faithful to him. Tell God you're a vehicle for him. If he wants you to do something, he'll let you know. It's your job to listen for instructions. Be kind and warm to people, especially your family and those closest to you, and you will find peace."

What are your thoughts about Mairead Maguire's advice on finding peace? Test her theory today by listening prayerfully for God's instructions. At the end of the day, write down what you heard and felt throughout the day.

Searching for Peace: Round Two

Prayerfulness invites peacefulness, which, in turn, invites God to share more information about our unique life purpose! We grow and learn as we spend time with God, which causes us to want to be obedient to his will. As we begin to understand our next immediate step, we don't feel as driven to have all the long-range answers. Step by step, our faith increases, and we learn to trust that God does have a plan for our lives.

Use this "Inner Peace Checklist" to evaluate your progress in pursuing peace.

Are You …

- Enjoying the company of God while you're doing chores such as the laundry or the dishes?
- Craving longer, more frequent, private appointments with the Holy Spirit?
- Finding peace about upcoming, difficult decisions by reading and meditating on biblical truths?
- Writing in a spiritual journal for the privilege of recording your conversations with God?
- Recognizing God at work, especially in your moments of anxiety and disquiet?
- Getting a good laugh out of the song, "I Did It My Way"?
- Teaching your children or others to listen to God—and being humbled by the life-changing results?

The Sojourner's Guide to Pursuing Peace

The following suggestions and activities will help you in your pursuit of inner peace. But before you consider working on the suggestions below, it might be a good idea to identify your starting point. Consider where you are on the Inner Peace Richter Scale:

Full-fledged frantic	Semi-serene	At peace

Why did you place yourself where you did on the scale above? What indications led you to that conclusion?

_____

_____

_____

_____

_____

_____

_____

_____

_____

_____

_____

_____

_____

_____

_____

1. Practice silence.

   Create opportunities for God to speak to you by practicing silence. Do your part by reducing noise, stimuli, and information overload. Ask God daily to make you a better listener. Ask him to take you from where you are today to where he always intended you to be. The more you practice quietness in your life, the more opportunities you will find to be silent before the Lord.

   Record here your thoughts, prayers, and any impressions you receive from the Lord during your quiet time.

2. Stop the endless mind chatter.

The path to peace is paved with long stretches of silence. Often, the most damaging noise comes from internal mind chatter. Do you constantly talk to yourself (silently or out loud)? If so, it's time to stop the brain noise. Stop torturing yourself. You don't have to be your own captive audience. Tell yourself to be quiet.

Use this page to write down some of the "chatter" that keeps you from true silence before the Lord. Record it as a way of getting it out of your head. Write a short prayer at the bottom of the page, asking God to take these things and lock them away so they won't rob you of the peace he wants you to have.

_____

_____

_____

_____

_____

_____

_____

_____

_____

_____

_____

_____

_____

_____

_____

_____

_____

_____

3. Shoot bullet prayers to heaven all day long.

    Train yourself in the habit of talking to and listening to God all day, every day. This week, try shooting off speeding-bullet prayers regarding everything you do. Then, slow down to enjoy God's replies. Expect answers on all aspects of your character development, roles, relationships, finances, purposes, and more.

    Record here some of the replies you hear from God in response to your bullet prayers.

    _____

    _____

    _____

    _____

    _____

    _____

    _____

    _____

    _____

    _____

    _____

    _____

    _____

    _____

4. Don't feel guilty about silence that puts you to sleep.

    If you are physically tired or emotionally exhausted, you may fall asleep while you're trying to listen to God. Not to worry. Resting is biblical. So if you need a nap, don't feel guilty. A nap can be an excellent, no-cost therapy for whatever is ailing you.

5. Purposely change your pace.

   Learn to slow down. Make a conscientious effort to eliminate the pressure of performing for a while. Slowing down greatly increases peacefulness.

   Take a moment to honestly list some things that you could cut out of your schedule that would allow you more time for quiet.

   _____

   _____

   _____

   _____

   _____

   _____

6. Avoid peace killers.

   Adjust your priorities to stay away from three top peace killers: people-pleasing, keeping up with the Joneses, and worrying about things that are out of your control. The next time you catch yourself in one of these traps, talk to a friend about holding you accountable to stop it.

   Write down some specific ways that you can avoid these peace killers in your own life.

   _____

   _____

   _____

   _____

   _____

   _____

Personal Pathway Questions

1. How well do you listen to God throughout the day?

    _____

    _____

    _____

2. Write anything you currently do that encourages you to pursue
    peace by listening to God. Consider the following list:

    • Quiet Time (reflection)
    • Prayer
    • Private or Community Worship (singing or instrumental music)
    • Journaling
    • Spiritual Fasting
    • Attitude of Constant Listening
    • Bible Study Time
    • Creating Silence
    • Reducing Busyness
    • Bullet Prayers

    _____

    _____

    _____

3. Which ideas from Question 2 would you like to experiment with
    to increase your desire to listen?

    _____

    _____

    _____

    _____

4. What makes it difficult for you to hear God? What can you do to lessen the difficulty?

_____

_____

_____

_____

_____

5. Did you realize before this chapter that pursuing peace is a God-intended purpose for your life? Or, that you can pursue peace by listening to God? What does this information teach a woman who says, "I just want to know what my life purpose is"?

_____

_____

_____

_____

_____

6. What is God nudging you to do about pursuing peace?

_____

_____

_____

_____

_____

God's Wisdom for the Pathway

The "Martha versus Mary" Step of Life:
Pursue Peace.

For a lesson from two sisters, Martha and Mary, read Luke 10:38-42. For many of us, this is a difficult story to hear, because we have so many responsibilities to juggle. On any given day, we are much more like Martha, busy serving others, and we forget that Jesus wants to spend time with us. Has busyness prevented you from being with the Lord? If so, how about starting today to seek his companionship and peace *in the midst of it all?*

Too often we are made to feel that "it's Mary's way or no way." The truth is that, in addition to sitting—uninterrupted—at our Lord's feet daily (like Mary), we also need to invite Jesus into all the hectic moments of our lives (which Martha was too frazzled to do). Just imagine Jesus hoping to be invited into Martha's kitchen for a long chat as they worked together.

How do you relate to the story of Mary and Martha? To which sister can you relate the most? Why? What can you learn from this passage that you can apply to your everyday life?

Repent of All Your Offenses

The stepping-stone *repent and turn away from all your offenses* causes many women to take a step of hesitation. What is it about repentance that makes us hesitate? Repentance requires that we honestly appraise our sin life and adjust our thoughts and deeds accordingly. It requires trusting God with our frailties and failures, persevering against temptation, practicing a prayerful lifestyle, and being willing to make deeply personal changes.

_____

_____

_____

_____

_____

_____

_____

_____

_____

_____

_____

_____

_____

_____

_____

> What are your feelings and concerns about taking the step of repentance? What do you find is the most difficult about repenting of sin?

Why Is Sin Such a Big Deal?

Sin is a deliberate turning away from God. Repentance is remorse or sincere contrition for our sinful conduct. It is regret and sorrow that lead to a willingness to change, and change makes all the difference. After we confess (or admit) our sin to God and turn away from it, our changed life turns us toward God. As we draw closer to God, we are better able to discover our life's purpose; as we discover our life's purpose, we draw closer to God. In contrast, sin will always push us away from God, away from his voice, and away from his purposes.

How have you seen sin push you away from God, his voice, and his purposes? Of what do you need to repent so that you can draw closer to God and better hear his plans for your purpose?

Stumbling over Sin

Women who are on track to pursue their life purpose make changes. They seek to follow the guidelines that will make them better vessels for God's use. They repent and invite God to remove weaknesses, stumbling blocks, and sins from their lives. This intentional discipline helps keep them free of excess baggage, garbage, and excuses for living poorly. It helps set them free to live a better life.

_____

_____

_____

_____

_____

_____

_____

_____

According to this description, are you on track to pursue your life purposes? Are you seeking God's help in ridding your life of sin? What excess baggage, garbage, or excuses do you need God to prune from your life right now?

Repentance: A Liberating Step

Repentance is one of the most liberating steps we can take in life, and it comes with so many benefits. When we confess and repent of our sin, we are forgiven and restored. Repentance delivers us from shame, guilt, anger, hopelessness, and bitterness. It releases us from slavery to sin and holds us captive to the desire for a deeper relationship with God. It sets us free to work in concert with God instead of against him, and it allows us to receive the best that God has so graciously planned for our lives.

What about you? Are you craving freedom from the things that keep you from living the life you were meant to live? If so, make a list of your stumbling blocks and sins, offer your list to God, and be willing to turn away from those temptations in the future.

The Sojourner's Guide to Practicing Repentance

Repentance is a practice that will become very familiar to us as we seek to hear from God about the unique purpose he has for each of us. The following suggestions will help you follow through and make great strides on your pathway to purpose.

1. Turn toward God.

   Do whatever it takes to invite God to work on you. Your Creator loves you and wants you to succeed on your life mission. Turn toward him and ask him to lead you to a Scripture, person, circumstance, or activity that will help you change your ways.

   Prayer, meditating on God's Word, seeking Christian counseling or therapy, Bible study, conversations with other Christians, and reading books about how to turn from the sins you struggle with are all things you can do to invite God to work in your life. What specific things will you plan to do this week to turn toward God?

   _____

   _____

   _____

   _____

   _____

   _____

   _____

   _____

   _____

   _____

   _____

   _____

2. Memorize a Scripture.

   You may want to memorize Romans 7:18, one of the most comforting Scripture passages on repentance: "I have the desire to do what is good, but I cannot carry it out." God knows how hard it is to change sin patterns. Just remember: you are responding to a God who loves you very much, not to a God who is angry with you for not being able to get it right the first time.

   Take some time to find several Scripture passages on repentance. Write them down and make some notes about any insights they give you. Pick two verses that especially speak to you. Memorize them this week.

   _____

   _____

   _____

   _____

   _____

   _____

   _____

   _____

   _____

   _____

   _____

   _____

   _____

   _____

   _____

   _____

   _____

   _____

3. Consider the consequences of your sin.

   The consequences of your sin can be widespread, even spilling over onto the next generation, such as when your children continue a sin cycle of abuse or addiction that they have seen in your life.

   Think for a moment about one confessed sin in your life. What were the positive results (obvious or hidden) of repenting of that sin?

   Now think of a current sin from which you have not repented. What might be the possible negative consequences of it?

   Ask God today to forgive you for that sin and free you from its power. Don't ask simply to avoid the potentially tough consequences, but ask for forgiveness because God is almighty, and he is waiting for you to repent.

   _____

   _____

   _____

   _____

   _____

   _____

   _____

   _____

   _____

   _____

   _____

   _____

   _____

4. Consider missed blessings.

   Sin also can cause you to miss out on blessings.

   Recall a past sin and ask yourself, *What blessing might I have missed because of it?* Then, think of a current sin from which you have not repented and identify what the potential missed blessings might be.

   _____

   _____

   _____

   _____

   _____

   _____

   _____

   _____

5. Accept reproof.

   Write a prayer asking the Holy Spirit to alert you to your sins and prepare your heart to hear and accept reproof or correction. In response to this prompt to stop sinning, flee from one temptation this week. Don't apologize to anyone about running away from the temptation, and don't look back—just run!

   _____

   _____

   _____

   _____

   _____

   _____

6. Be honest with yourself about five sins.

    Use the list below to identify some of your sin tendencies and evaluate your readiness to carry out God's will for your life. This exercise will help you see the truth about whether or not you are cooperating with God's plan to the fullest. Enlist the help of an objective friend as needed.

Five Sins That Distract You from God's Best for Your Life:

    1. Jealousy
    2. Anger
    3. Pride
    4. Disobedience
    5. Dishonesty

    _____

    _____

    _____

    _____

    _____

    _____

    _____

    _____

7. Pray this prayer.

    Lord, I know that because I'm human, I will still continue to sin, but please reduce the time it takes me to recognize and repent of sins like anger, disobedience, pride, or greed. If it used to take me a week to recognize and repent of a sin, let it take me one day, one hour, one minute, or one second instead. I don't want my sin to cause me to offend you or rob you of my obedience. Please strengthen me now. In Jesus' precious name I pray. Amen.

Personal Pathway Questions

1. How often do you confess your sins to God?

    _____

    _____

    _____

    _____

2. Write anything that prompts you to repent. Here are some
    examples:

    Knowing that Jesus has forgiven me
    Reproof or correction from someone I trust and love
    A scripture verse that speaks to my heart
    Getting caught; being embarrassed

    _____

    _____

    _____

    _____

3. Which ideas from Question 2 will you use now to increase your
    desire to confess and repent?

    _____

    _____

    _____

    _____

    _____

    _____

4. What is God nudging you to do about offering one particular weakness to him?

_____

_____

_____

_____

_____

_____

_____

_____

_____

5. "Let us throw off everything that hinders and the sin that so easily entangles, and let us run with perseverance the race marked out for us" (Hebrews 12:1). What is your response to this verse?

_____

_____

_____

_____

_____

_____

_____

_____

_____

God's Wisdom for the Pathway

The "Samaritan Woman's" Step of Life:
Repenting and Turning Away from All Your Offenses.

For a lesson from the Samaritan woman on taking a step toward repentance, read John 4:7-42. Jesus spoke with her when she went to draw water from a well. He told her that he knew she had had five husbands and was now with a man who was not her husband. After he revealed himself to her as the Messiah of the world, she became an evangelist, pointing those in her town to Jesus.

Your repentance over sin may or may not involve a dramatic conversion like that of the woman at the well, but with what sin or character issue are you struggling? Will you repent now and turn away from your offense?

_____

_____

_____

_____

_____

_____

_____

_____

_____

_____

_____

_____

_____

_____

_____

Go the Extra Mile

Wash One Another's Feet

The stepping-stone, *wash one another's feet,* sends some of us into a crying, whining fit. No matter how much we complain about the high expectations of this servant's step, God has never chosen to recall this stepping-stone. It may not appeal to us, but in God's eyes this stone is beautiful. Humble ser-vice may not make our priority list, it may not be popular with the masses, but it is what God desires.

_____

_____

_____

_____

_____

_____

_____

> What are your feelings about being a humble servant? What about this stepping-stone causes you to struggle? What do you think is at the root of your feelings about service?

A Requirement with Rich Rewards

Serving others is very satisfying and rewarding. Washing one another's feet gives us a mini-purpose for today. In addition, humble service in daily things quite often leads to service in a broader arena. Faithful service also yields the reward of learning empathy and patience as you move toward fulfilling your life purpose. As you partner with God in serving others, you'll learn to depend on him as the source and strength behind your particular assignments and giftedness.

Have you ever experienced any of the benefits mentioned above from acts of service you have done? If you have, journal about that experience and its impact on your life. If you haven't, journal about why you might have missed out on these benefits so far.

Don't Be Afraid of Your Faltering Steps

God can use any service adventure, easy or difficult, to help us recognize our need for spiritual maturity. And if we are ever to fulfill and relish our God-ordained purposes in life, we must mature spiritually. That's why the stepping-stone of serving others is so important. Our steps toward serving others, however wavering they may be at first, are crucial to our becoming women of purpose.

When have you felt awkward and unsure when you have tried to serve? What was the outcome? Did you learn from the experience in spite of being uncomfortable? How does it make you feel to know that God honors even faltering steps of service?

Obedience Testing 101

God may nudge us to serve in an area of our preference because he wants us to get used to the idea of ministering to others. He may give us the option of moving in and out of service opportunities of our own choosing. This allows us to discover for ourselves the ministries we prefer and those for which we are best equipped. Before long, we will find ministries that match our passions. We will realize that it is a treat and a privilege to serve.

_____

_____

_____

_____

_____

_____

_____

_____

_____

_____

What ministry opportunities could you investigate right now that would fit into your own gifts and passions? Write down some activities you enjoy or areas of giftedness you see in your life. Imagine what ministries could use your abilities and write them here.

_____

_____

_____

_____

Obedience Testing—The Graduate Course

Sometimes God asks us to serve in an assignment that is way outside our comfort zone or area of giftedness. He may do this to stretch our faith or to teach us a valuable lesson. It is often hard to follow God's instructions, and I know that we will fail sometimes in our efforts to become faithful servants. But let's help eachother remember that, serving others is an act of obedience to the one who paid for our every act of disobedience by his death on the cross.

_____

_____

_____

_____

_____

_____

_____

_____

_____

_____

_____

_____

_____

_____

_____

> What ministries are outside of your comfort zone? Have you ever allowed God to stretch you by ministering in a way that is difficult for you? What are your feelings about opening yourself to the possibility of obeying God in a ministry that makes you uncomfortable?

The Sojourner's Guide to Foot Washing

The following suggestions will help you discover opportunities to obey God's leading as he directs you on your path of service. Take as much time on this step as you need. Ministering to others will eventually become a natural part of your everyday life. I'm still pluggin along, day by day.

1. Seize an opportunity to give yourself away today.

    Ask God what opportunity he would like you to seize today to give yourself (your energy, time, and/or resources) away. Then volunteer for the next service moment he puts in your pathway. Tell God you want him to use you—whenever, wherever, and however—and see where the adventure takes you!

    List some ministry opportunities that you would like to explore and what steps you are going to take to get involved in them.

    _____

    _____

    _____

    _____

    _____

    _____

    _____

    _____

    _____

    _____

    _____

    _____

    _____

    _____

2. Think long term.

   What is God leading you to do for him in the long term? Does he want you to join the benevolence team at your church, go on a mission trip, or help start a church? Whether God reveals a suggestion that takes you into your local community or around the world, consider a long-term ministry perspective that will impact your service commitment forever.

   Take some time to listen for what God might want to say to you about your long-term ministry. Write down what you hear and your concerns, thoughts, and feelings about these possibilities. Use this exercise as your first step in exploring what God has for your future in his service.

   _____

   _____

   _____

   _____

   _____

   _____

   _____

   _____

   _____

   _____

   _____

   _____

   _____

   _____

   _____

   _____

3. Stay balanced; retain some margin.

   Don't overload your schedule with service commitments that exceed the healthy limitations of your life. You are the only one who can keep your service ship from sinking. On the other hand, don't hide behind self-created busyness as an excuse not to serve. Discard everything that could distract you from a course of service.

   Give some serious thought to your schedule. Are you overloaded in some areas? Are there things you could cut out of your schedule that would lessen the load and allow more time for service to others? Ask God to give you his eyes as you look at your priorities.

   _____

   _____

   _____

   _____

   _____

   _____

   _____

   _____

   _____

   _____

   _____

   _____

   _____

   _____

   _____

   _____

   _____

4. Take a test.

   Take a spiritual gifts inventory like Discovering Your Spiritual Gifts *by Kenneth Kinghorn to see if you can identify your top three spiritual gifts. Then, spend some time investigating and reflecting on the possible applications of those gifts.*

   Record what you discover about your spiritual gifts here. Use this page to write out some ideas on how you can use the gifts God has given you.

   _____

   _____

   _____

   _____

   _____

   _____

   _____

   _____

   _____

   _____

   _____

   _____

   _____

   _____

   _____

   _____

   _____

   _____

   _____

5. Try on new ministry shoes.

   The concept of trying on different "giftedness shoes" to see which ones God designed for you to wear can be helpful. Take a look in God's ministry closet. Go ahead—try on the shoes! Clomp around some. Give yourself permission to fall down. You'll need to practice walking through some anxiety or uncertainty, which will help you develop new skills and insights. In time, you'll learn to recognize whether or not certain ministry shoes are a good or perfect fit.

   What "ministry shoes" would you like to try on for size? List a few ideas, and make a plan to try them on soon.

   _____

   _____

   _____

   _____

   _____

   _____

   _____

   _____

   _____

   _____

   _____

   _____

   _____

   _____

   _____

   _____

Personal Pathway Questions

1. In what ways do you typically submit to God's plan of service for your life each day?

_____

_____

_____

_____

_____

2. What holds you back from acts of service? What solution comes to mind to remedy these hindrances?

_____

_____

_____

_____

_____

3. List as many church, community, and world mission assignments in which you can remember participating over the years. Put "LF" by several of your **L**east **F**avorite or "MF" by several of your **M**ost **F**avorite service commitments.

_____

_____

_____

_____

_____

4. What is one step you could take toward service today (for example, make a phone call, do some research on a topic, meet with a ministry leader, take a class, start serving)?

_____

_____

_____

_____

_____

_____

_____

_____

_____

_____

_____

_____

_____

_____

_____

_____

_____

_____

_____

_____

_____

_____

God's Wisdom for the Pathway

The "Dorcas" Step of Life:
Washing One Another's Feet.

For a lesson from Dorcas, beloved servant to her friends, read Acts 9:36-42.
Mourners packed into a room to grieve the loss of Dorcas when she died.
She was a kind woman who had made a great impact on her community by
her gift of *helps*.

_____

_____

_____

_____

_____

_____

_____

What legacy of unselfish service will you leave? Will you follow where God is leading you today? What might be holding you back from using your God-given gifts to the fullest?

Write a prayer asking God to help you discover, unwrap, and use the wonderful gifts he has given you. If you need help getting started, use this prayer as a model for your own:

Lord, I know that service is a disposition—an attitude of my heart, an availability of my spirit. When I allow you to empty my heart of selfish pride, I make room for you to enter. Though you are rich, you willingly emptied yourself out of love for me, becoming a humble servant. Help me become more like you.

_____

_____

_____

_____

_____

_____

_____

_____

_____

_____

_____

_____

_____

_____

_____

_____

_____

_____

_____

_____

_____

_____

Walk with Integrity

Caution ahead! You will need prayer, balance, and concentration to avoid being thrown off this next stepping-stone: *Walk with integrity, not duplicity.* Integrity can be defined as oneness between our mind and actions, or unity of our thoughts and deeds. Our integrity determines whether we halfheartedly or fully participate in God's best purposes for our lives. Authentic living with genuine integrity bonds our hearts with the very heart of God.

Do you feel that you live your life with integrity? Why or why not? What evidence in your life makes you think this way?

Integrity versus Duplicity

A woman of integrity thinks what she says she thinks, feels what she says she feels, and does what she says she will do. She keeps the promises she makes. Her motives are pure. She is honest, upright, and genuine. She is real in her relationships. A woman of duplicity has the ability, like a seasoned poker player, to convey messages through her words or actions that are opposite of her inner thoughts or planned actions. What is actually in her heart or on her mind would surprise you.

Which of these women describes you? Write down some specific examples from your own life that show what kind of woman you are.

So, What's the Big Deal?

God is all-knowing and everywhere present. No façades or false motives can be hidden from him. He hates it when our secret motive is, for example, to manipulate a situation, control an opinion, seek revenge, stir up trouble, embarrass someone, or show off. Those things are destructive to our relationships with him and with others. God knows that living without integrity will inevitably destroy us, as well as destroy our relationships. Duplicity has no place in God's purposes.

> What impure motives are you embarrassed to admit you have? How have these motives caused problems in your own heart and in your relationships with others? How do you feel, knowing that you cannot hide them from God?

God Can Use Impure Motives

This may come as a shock to you, but God can use impure motives. Years ago my daughter Stephanie reluctantly agreed to sing at a senior center only because I insisted she do so. In spite of my control-driven motivation and Steph's compliance-driven motivation, God still used the experience poignantly. He revealed to her a true desire for using her voice to serve God's people. He gave her a taste of putting love into action and being changed by ministry.

> How have you seen God use your impure motives or those of others for his good purposes? What does this say to you about the character of God?

God Isn't Interested in Ministry-by-Guilt

Ministry-by-guilt is a common motivational misstep that throws many women off balance, and they may not even understand why. How many times, for example, have you served with a fake smile because of the haunting words *should* or *supposed to*? If you hear yourself using those words when you are making a decision, it can be a warning sign that you need to take time out for a motive check.

When have you served or ministered because of guilt? What was the source of the guilt you felt? Do you think your motive affected the quality of your service?

Self-Test for Walking with Integrity

So, how do we become women of integrity? Integrity requires a willingness to inspect closely the motives for our actions. Is our motive, for example, to impress someone, get sympathy, avoid embarrassment, or make people more like us? We need to learn to check our motives for everything we do—from mentoring to committee work, from classroom volunteering to visiting a lonely neighbor. We test our motives by regularly asking ourselves one simple question: *Why am I doing this?*

_____

_____

_____

_____

_____

_____

_____

_____

List a few ministries or volunteer obligations in which you are involved right now. For each one, honestly ask yourself, *Why am I doing this?* and write down what you truly feel your motivations are.

_____

_____

_____

_____

_____

_____

_____

The Impact of Integrity

When it is our determined purpose to learn to be women of integrity and pure motives, not only do we begin to think differently, we also will act, talk, pray, and serve in a different manner. A woman of integrity can look herself in the mirror and say, "I am who I say I am." She will be able to hold her head up and look people in the eye. No more hiding, pretending, or guilt. No more burnout from the exhausting drain of hidden motives. *That* peace of mind alone is worth the effort!

_____

_____

_____

_____

_____

_____

_____

_____

_____

_____

_____

_____

_____

_____

Write a prayer expressing your desire for integrity in your life. Ask God to help you in the areas that you struggle the most. He is always willing to give you a fresh start when you ask!

The Sojourner's Guide to Walking with Integrity

The following suggestions are designed to help you evaluate your integrity and sort out your motives as you seek to discover and fulfill God's purposes in your life.

1. Ask God for a specific example.

   Ask God to show you a specific instance when you were double-minded. Then confess it to the Lord and repent. If you have been living a fragmented life of lies and duplicity, trust that God will rejoice in your willingness to talk to him about it.

   Write down any instances of double-mindedness or duplicity that God brings to your mind during this exercise. Then ask for his forgiveness. As you confess and repent of each one, mark them out as a visible reminder that God is taking your sin away.

2. Ask a friend for specifics.

   Once you have asked for forgiveness for your duplicity, repentance requires that you set up some boundaries for yourself in this area. Look for one trustworthy, safe individual with whom you feel comfortable talking. Schedule a conversation about integrity, authenticity, and duplicity. Get real with your plans to offer your weaknesses to God.

   Use this page to record the insights you receive from this conversation.

_____

_____

_____

_____

_____

_____

_____

_____

_____

_____

_____

_____

_____

_____

_____

_____

_____

_____

3. Offer your impure motives to God.

   If you have a favorite unhealthy motive such as pity, profit, or reward, offer that impure motive to God so he can purify it.

   What is your motive for wanting God to give you an important life purpose? Set aside time in your schedule this week to offer God any of your impure motives related to your purpose, ministry, or life mission.

   _____

   _____

   _____

   _____

   _____

   _____

   _____

   _____

   _____

   _____

   _____

   _____

   _____

   _____

   _____

   _____

   _____

   _____

   _____

   _____

Personal Pathway Questions

1. Think about a time when a lack of integrity led you to cheating, envy, slander, scheming, malice, flattery, treachery, secret wickedness, duplicity, vain conceit, selfish ambition, or some other sin. Talk to God about how you now feel about the situation. Ask him to forgive you, if you have never done so before.

_____

_____

_____

_____

_____

_____

_____

_____

_____

_____

_____

_____

_____

_____

_____

_____

_____

_____

_____

2. What is your primary reason for service? Give some in-depth thought to why you serve. Think about Jesus' compassion and humility when he served others, but most of all, meditate on his selfless, loving sacrifice on the cross.

_____

_____

_____

_____

_____

_____

_____

_____

_____

_____

_____

_____

_____

_____

_____

_____

_____

_____

_____

_____

_____

_____

_____

3. To begin to live a more authentic life of integrity, take this opportunity to question your motives for any of your routine actions, such as giving a gift, making a prayer request, going to a social gathering, offering to help someone, supporting a cause, giving a speech, volunteering at your church office, or making a large purchase for yourself. Create and record them on a simple chart, like this:

My Pure Motives	My Impure Motives

4. What thoughts do you have about your lists in Question 3? Confess any duplicity, and pray for God to instill a love for integrity in your heart.

_____

_____

_____

_____

_____

_____

_____

_____

God's Wisdom for the Pathway

The "Miriam" Step of Life:
Walk with Integrity, Not Duplicity.

For a lesson of what happened to Miriam, Moses' sister, when she hid improper motives, read Numbers 12. Miriam was jealous of Moses' influence and power. God knew that. Instead of being humbly honest with God about her envy, Miriam's wounded pride caused her to criticize Moses' wife. Her motives: to discredit Moses and to attempt to feel better about herself by causing people to think less of him. God dealt severely with her jealous, ego-laden efforts to dishonor his chosen messenger.

What is one of your secret, impure motives? If you can't think of any, Psalm 139:23-24 is a good prayer to use to invite God's inspection: "Search me, O God, and know my heart; test me and know my anxious thoughts. See if there is any offensive way in me, and lead me in the way everlasting."

Run to Jesus

Expect the Desires of Your Heart

For many women, the next stepping-stone will appear to be a welcome relief: the step of *expecting God to give you the desires of your heart.* Yet, an uneasiness that you don't understand may also start to build within you.

• You fear you will end up disappointed.

• Perhaps you find yourself wondering, *Maybe this stepping-stone is one of Satan's traps to coax me into wanting worldly rewards.*

• Or you worry that you are selfish. If you are truly honest with yourself, you may have to admit that your deepest desires have much more to do with your own happiness than with God's purposes and your holiness.

Can you identify with any of these worries about expecting your heart's desire? Write about your thoughts and feelings when it comes to expecting good things from God.

Your Passion—It's a God Thing

Let me assure you, this stepping-stone is *not* a trap in disguise. The psalmist David spells out the win-win nature of this step in Psalm 37:4. I like to explain its general message like this:

If you will make God the chief affection of your inmost heart . . . [Meaning you delight yourself in the Lord, find enormous pleasure and joy in him, get to know him well by continually sitting in his presence and obeying him],

He will give you the desires of your heart. [Meaning you will receive boundless enthusiasm for the deep passions, cravings, longings, petitions, and aspirations that he planted in your heart.]

God wants you, his daughter, to have the desires of your heart.

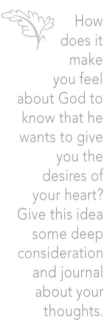

How does it make you feel about God to know that he wants to give you the desires of your heart? Give this idea some deep consideration and journal about your thoughts.

Unwrap God's Gift of Passion

Our passion reflects our deepest yearnings. It underscores the beauty we crave, such as art or music, and reflects our need for such intangibles as freedom or adventure. It can be an expression of our most important drives. Passion can be so powerful that it seems to have a life of its own. Unbidden, it can lead us to lose ourselves for hours in a fascinating world where time seems to stand still.

What do the desires of your heart look like? Does your greatest passion manifest itself in the form of a hobby, your career, or volunteer work? Is it best fulfilled through a contribution you'd like to make to society? Or is it tied in with your lifestyle, with your personal longing to be married, to travel, or to follow some other dream?

Regardless of what your passion is, God gave it to you and made you his steward of it. So, why not go ahead and live with the desires and purpose your Creator intended you to have? God wants to use every part of you, including the passions he chose for you and stirs within you. He wants your passion to be alive and well and available to him whenever he wants to use it for his purposes.

What passions are you already pursuing? What passions have you been afraid to pursue? Take some time to write about your hopes and dreams, asking God to show you how they might be realized as part of his purpose for you.

Passion That Sizzles

Where has your passion shown up through the varied seasons of your life?
As a child, were you passionate about raising an animal, reading detective
stories, or drawing? As a teen or young adult, were you passionate about
environmental issues, playing volleyball, or getting straight As in high
school? As an adult, have you been passionate about having a child,
building Habitat for Humanity houses, or teaching English as a second
language?

_____

_____

_____

_____

_____

_____

_____

_____

_____

_____

_____

_____

What have you done
with those passions?
God gave them to
you for a purpose—
to be used for his
glory and his plans.
Will you join
him in that
purpose?

_____

_____

_____

_____

What? No Passion?

All of us go through dry spells and tough seasons of life when our passions take a back seat. God, who created you and watches over you, sees all that is happening in your life. He knows your obligations and commitments and why you may have put your passions on temporary hold. He knows when fear, guilt, shattered dreams, fatigue, a broken heart, or heavy responsibilities may be hiding the desires of your heart from view.

If this is your situation, ask God to use his intimate knowledge of you to draw you closer to him, to heal you, to strengthen you, and to help you trust him more. Ask him to take you—when the timing is right—from the dispassionate place you are right now to a passionate place that holds great joy for you.

How Will You Fill the Passion Void?

A lack of passion can quickly turn into a serious problem, especially if we attempt to fill that void with unhealthy passions. If we want to truly experience the desires of our heart and discover God's purposes, we must guard against the seductive power of unhealthy passions. Let healthy, God-given passions help protect you against unhealthy ones. Tell God you want the Spirit-filled passions he instilled in you, not the harmful ones you could import.

_____

_____

_____

_____

_____

_____

_____

_____

_____

_____

_____

_____

_____

_____

_____

_____

_____

What unhealthy passions (alcohol, overeating, compulsive spending, watching too much TV) are most seductive to you? With what God-given passions can you replace them, so that you fill your passion void in a godly way?

Look Forward to What God Will Do

My top five passions are:

    1. A heart for women

    2. Sherlock Holmes mysteries

    3. Jigsaw puzzles

    4. Finding life's purpose

    5. Travel

So, what perfect purpose did God graciously orchestrate for me out of the sheer goodness of his heart? I help women put the mysterious puzzles of their lives together by encouraging them to reflect on their current and long-term purposes. And, as a speaker and missionary to women around the world, I travel.

_____

_____

_____

_____

_____

_____

_____

> What are your top five passions? How might God orchestrate them in your life to fulfill his ultimate purpose for you? Take some time to dream some big dreams as you journal about your passions!

_____

_____

_____

_____

The Sojourner's Guide to Delighting in Your Passions

The following suggestions are designed to help you find and nurture the God-given desires of your heart. Start today, but be careful not to rush the process. Take as much time as you need to uncover your passions and discover how they flow into God's purposes for your life.

1. Some basic hints to get started.

   To get a clear picture of the desires of your heart, try out several of the following ideas that have proven helpful to women over the years:

   • Hang around passionate people.

   • Ask family and friends what they've noticed about your desires or potential passions.

   • Get out of your rut! Do something different, unusual, out of your normal routine. Do whatever is needed to get you out of your humdrum box and inspire you to think beyond your daily grind.

   • Once you recognize several of your passions, dedicate them to God—and enjoy them.

   Write about your times of greatest joy, regardless of their size, scope, or nature. Ask God to reveal any desires and passions that might be related to those times of joy.

   _____

   _____

   _____

   _____

   _____

   _____

   _____

2. Guard against jealousy.

   Guard against jealousy of other people's desires, dreams, and passionate assignments from God. Fight diligently against envy: Track it, expose it, hate it, renounce it, and flee from it. One of the best ways I have found to do this is to help others fulfill their exciting dreams. Pray for them, encourage them, assist them, introduce them to people who can cheer them on, share your resources with them, and coach them.

   Of whom are you tempted to be jealous because of their assignment from God? In order to combat that jealousy how can you get involved in helping them fulfill their dream?

   _____

   _____

   _____

   _____

   _____

   _____

   _____

   _____

   _____

   _____

   _____

   _____

   _____

   _____

   _____

   _____

3. Daydream.

   Whether or not you are ready for a new career or ministry today, spend some time thinking about one that would ignite your passion. Daydream about it as if the sky were the limit. This exercise will give you an out-of-the-box perspective.

   Let your imagination soar and write down any big or little dream that comes to you. Ask God to show you a desire or passion that you could begin to investigate when the time is right.

   _____

   _____

   _____

   _____

   _____

   _____

   _____

   _____

   _____

   _____

   _____

   _____

   _____

   _____

4. Go for it!

   Experiment. Follow your hunches until you feel passionate about something that's legal, moral, and ethical. Let the process take as long as it needs to take. Don't rush the discovery.

Personal Pathway Questions

Look at your passions in several categories: as a hobby you love, a personal longing you have, a group or cause you want to help, or a contribution you'd love to make. This simple mechanism will help you think of answers to the question, "What are you passionate about?" from four different perspectives.

1. What *hobby* are you passionate about?

    Snorkeling   Quilting   Collecting antiques   Fishing
    Mountain climbing   Baseball   Gourmet cooking   Reading

    Other: _____

    _____

2. What personal *longing or hope* are you passionate about?

    Financial security   Marriage   Having children   Travel
    Screenplay contract   Country house with a white picket fence
    Private counseling practice

    Other: _____

    _____

3. For what *group or cause* do you have a passionate ache in your heart?

    Illiterate   Elderly   Immigrants   Unemployed
    Pro-life   Rain forests   Endangered species   Justice

    Other: _____

    _____

4. What passionate *contribution* do you dream about making?

    Lobbying for handicap rights   Starting a choir

    Evangelizing movie producers   Feeding the homeless

    Becoming a short-term missionary

    Other: _____

    _____

5. Looking back over your answers to Questions 1-4, in what way
    might God purposefully use one or more of your passions to give
    you a unique kingdom-building assignment? There are no wrong
    answers. Let your creativity take over.

    _____

    _____

    _____

    _____

    _____

    _____

    _____

    _____

    _____

    _____

    _____

    _____

    _____

    _____

    _____

    _____

God's Wisdom for the Pathway

The "Hannah" Step of Life:
Expect God to Give You the Desires of Your Heart.

For a lesson from Hannah during this step of your life, read 1 Samuel 1:1-2,
11. Hannah so passionately wanted a son that she tearfully poured her heart
out to the Lord in prayer, saying that if God blessed her with a son, she
would dedicate him to the Lord's service. Eli, a priest who was watching
Hannah pray, said to her: "Go in peace, and may the God of Israel grant you
what you have asked of him" (v. 17). Later, Hannah conceived Samuel. After
he was weaned, she took him to the temple to live.

Are you as passionate about something as Hannah was? Will you surrender your passion to the Lord to do with as he chooses?

Surrender Your Daily Life to God

The next stepping-stone, *surrender your everyday, ordinary life to God
as an offering,* isn't one step at all; it is a closely clustered group of small
stepping-stones. The process of taking many incremental steps of surrender
actually makes it easier to carefully consider each decision you make to
offer your life to God. Furthermore, the size of the stepping-stone is not
a true indicator of how difficult the step will be or how far it will take you.
But, once taken, even the smallest steps of surrender will cause you to develop quickly in your faith.

What are your thoughts
about surrendering your
life to God? Why do you
think this step along
the pathway
involves many
small steps?

Why Is Surrender So Important?

We simply cannot fulfill God's greatest purpose for us without surrendering our will and life to him. Surrender is essential to our *sanctification*, which is the never-ending process by which we are freed from sin and set apart for God's work and purposes. Surrender is about learning to live for an audience of one, and that is God. It means we let go of everything that takes a higher priority than God.

_____

_____

_____

_____

_____

_____

_____

_____

_____

_____

_____

Take some time to think about your priorities. Does anything take higher priority than God in your life? Are you willing to surrender those things in order to continue on the pathway to purpose?

_____

_____

_____

_____

_____

So, How Do We "Do" Surrender?

God provides surrender opportunities in many different ways, so we have to learn to recognize them. The Holy Spirit will always, in some way, prompt you to surrender and give you the opportunity to decide how to respond. God may ask you to turn over control of your goals and future plans. He may ask you to trust him with your fears, longings, or relationships. He may ask you to give him things as diverse as your addiction to sweets, your desire to be popular, your escalating credit-card debt, your old life scripts, or your most favored possessions.

What can you do this week to be more aware of the Holy Spirit's leading in the area of surrender? What things might he be prompting you to surrender even today?

God's Rich Rewards for Surrender

1. As you surrender to God, he begins to transform your life. The result of a transformed life is that you experience the precious blessings of his Spirit: "love, joy, peace, patience, kindness, goodness, faithfulness, gentleness and self control" (Galatians 5:22-23).

2. In addition, he will give you all the wisdom and focus you need to live a life of worship, gratitude, service, and purpose.

3. When you humbly give up your way and do whatever God asks of you, big or small, you please the God of the universe who promises never to desert you.

_____

_____

_____

_____

_____

> Are these rewards enough to inspire you toward surrender? Do you think that the difficulty of surrender is really worth the great rewards promised? Why or why not? With what do you most struggle when it comes to surrendering your life to Christ?

_____

_____

_____

_____

_____

_____

_____

The Longest Step of All

During a message that Kay Warren, my pastor's wife, gave at a church conference, she raised a tough question related to surrender. She asked if we would still follow God even if he never did another thing for us. *What if God didn't help me with my big dream of making a difference in the world? Would I still follow him?*

_____

_____

_____

_____

_____

_____

_____

_____

You, too, have the same choice. Will you take a step of surrender? Will you choose to follow God even if he never does another thing for you? Allow yourself to be completely honest as you journal about this difficult question.

Pathway to Purpose *for women*

The Sojourner's Guide to Step-by-Step Surrender

The following action steps for surrender will help you discover areas of your life God wants you to surrender to him. Practice these action steps for the next ten days to establish some new habits that will help you move forward on the pathway to purpose.

The Ten-Day Challenge

Revelation-Seek the Truth: Ask the Holy Spirit to show up during this ten-day process to reveal the truth to you about any relationship, situation, possession, feeling, or activity that may be blocking you from fulfilling your purposes on earth.

Investigation-Do Your Footwork and Homework: Make a phone call, read a book, talk with a Christian counselor, and/or attend an appropriate conference. Keep asking questions and pursuing answers until you come to a conclusion about your next step of surrender.

Calculation-Count the Cost: Evaluate what might change if God decides to take what you have surrendered. Prepare yourself to actually let go of what you say you are surrendering.

Transformation-Think with the Mind of Christ: Set your sights on becoming more like Christ. Focus on him and ask him to transform your thinking. Study appropriate scripture passages as you surrender a particular area of your life.

Declaration-Publicly Give Up Control of Your Will: Because surrender is an act of your will, not a function of your emotions or feelings, write an official declaration of your chosen course of action. Then, state your decision to another Christian and ask that person to hold you accountable.

Dedication-Prayerfully Begin: Surround yourself with one or more prayer warriors who will commit to pray that you will actually do the surrendering!

Record your progress in the Ten-Day Challenge on these pages.

The One-Day Challenge

If all of this seems too hard for you right now, take a "One-Day Surrender Challenge." Prayerfully and purposefully choose to surrender one thing that has a hold over you (anything from coffee to television to the telephone!) for twenty-four hours. Watch for and record any blessings that result in your relationships, energy level, attitude, or other areas.

_____

_____

_____

_____

_____

_____

_____

_____

_____

_____

_____

_____

_____

_____

_____

_____

_____

_____

_____

_____

Personal Pathway Questions

1. Describe one of your surrender journeys thus far with a particular person, place, thing, emotion, or issue. What has it taught you about God and yourself?

_____

_____

_____

_____

_____

_____

2. What is God nudging you to do about surrendering to him? (Is it to seek the truth; do your footwork and homework; count the cost; think with the mind of Christ; publicly give up control of your will; and/or prayerfully begin?) Why do you say that?

_____

_____

_____

_____

_____

_____

_____

_____

3. How would you complete this sentence and why? *I am ready to surrender both the good and bad parts of my life to God, including my _____.* (Consider your house, car, career, ministry, family, children, past, present, future, dreams, finances, addictions, fears, distractions, sins, hobbies, projects, fame, material possessions, power, reputation, spiritual growth, community work, friends, dark secrets, education.)

_____

_____

_____

_____

_____

_____

_____

_____

_____

_____

_____

_____

_____

Regardless of whether you surrendered anything today or not, you may want to say this prayer:

Lord, please take me from where I am today. You are acutely aware of how important _____ is/are to me. Help me to trust and obey you on a daily, hourly, and minute-by-minute basis.

God's Wisdom for the Pathway

The "Mary, Mother of Jesus" Step of Life:
Surrendering Your Everyday, Ordinary Life to God.

For a lesson from Mary, the mother of Jesus, read Luke 1:26-38. Mary's life was turned upside down the day an angel appeared to her with the news that she would be the mother of the Savior of the world. When she said yes to the angel, she was agreeing to let the Holy Spirit use her for God's glory. Did you know that she could have been stoned to death for being pregnant out of wedlock?

If God had asked you, instead of Mary, to surrender all your plans and dreams for a comfortable life and risk being stoned to death (or any other gruesome method of dying), what would you have said? Ask yourself, *What am I refusing to surrender to God today?* and then pray about dedicating that to the Almighty.

Point Others Toward the Pathway

Anticipate God's Vision

The next stepping-stone, *eagerly anticipate that the Lord God Almighty will reveal his vision to you*, is actually my favorite one along the pathway to purpose. I get excited about it because every woman has a unique, custom-made, broad-reach life purpose, and God wants to reveal his thoughts about it to her. It is nothing less than thrilling when a woman catches sight of God's vision and begins to intentionally live out her God-ordained life purpose.

You must be brave to prepare yourself to receive a vision, ask God to reveal it, admit when you have seen it, seek advice amid the confusion, and complete the work after you have your instructions. What feelings do you have about each of these big steps? What are your fears? What are your hopes?

God Will Reveal His Vision!

God's unique vision for you can be described as a desire that steals your heart. It is how you, and you alone, will minister with excellence in the eyes of the Lord. When you receive such a vision, you see an opportunity that so draws you to it that you can't stay away from it.

_____

_____

_____

_____

_____

_____

_____

_____

_____

_____

_____

_____

What hints have you received about God's vision for your specific life purpose? What passions has he given you? What opportunities have come your way? What are you drawn to and compelled by?

_____

_____

_____

_____

_____

_____

When you discern God's vision for your life, you may be utterly stunned, because fulfilling it will require tremendous faith, hope, and love. God's purpose will cost you your life in the sense that you must choose to die to self and accept his plan. Yet once vision is unleashed, it is like electricity that brings light to dark places. It is your personalized way of leading people from emptiness to surrender to significance in Christ. How amazing it is to look forward to God's vision!

_____

_____

_____

_____

_____

_____

_____

_____

_____

_____

_____

_____

_____

_____

Why do you think that God's vision for your life is always stunning and stretching? How might the specific desires and passions of your heart be like "electricity that brings light to dark places"?

Eager for Vision?

Anticipating God's vision can also haunt you with troubling "What if?" questions. *What if I am doing something wrong that is preventing God from speaking to me? What if God already revealed his vision to me, and I missed it? What if I heard God's thoughts, but I don't want to do what he told me to do?*

If these or similar questions are bogging you down, do yourself a huge favor and give yourself a fresh start. Put your past, with its doubts and failures, behind you, and consider today as the first day of the rest of your life to live for God.

What questions still trouble you about finding your God-given purpose? Journal about them and then write a prayer, giving your concerns to the Lord and asking him to give you a fresh start today.

Worth the Wait

If you are feeling impatient because of a long silence from God regarding his vision for your life, I have several suggestions.

1. Confess and repent of your impatience.
2. Thank God for his wisdom in teaching you to wait for his good timing.
3. Pay attention to what God is doing in your life today. What he is doing today may directly support and prepare you for the vision he will reveal to you tomorrow.

Consider the routine, daily purposes listed on the "Daily Purposes" side of the chart below. Pray that the Lord will reveal to you how your own daily purposes relate to his ultimate vision for you.

Daily Purposes	God's Ultimate Vision
Ministering to one or some	Ministering to some or multitudes
Expecting a tough assignment	Expecting God's intervention to complete an impossible assignment
Praying, *Use me, God!*	Praying boldly, *Use me up, God!*
Playing it safe and sure	Risking all, no holds barred
Handling daily tasks-at-hand in a Christlike manner	Carrying out your unique purpose in life filled with the fruit of the Spirit-love, joy, peace, patience, and so on (Gal. 5:22-23)

Vision Requires Action

No matter how or when God's vision comes to you, your ideal response to the concept would be complete surrender followed by action. Many Christian women remain frozen in a state of inaction when it is time to actually accept God's call on their lives. Of course, our vision will be scary; a vision is supposed to be bigger than life, more demanding than we know how to handle. God is not looking for "superstars" to whom he can reveal a vision. He is looking for dedicated, ordinary women who hold such a firm conviction about their unique purpose that they will doggedly persevere under trial.

_____

_____

_____

_____

_____

_____

_____

_____

_____

_____

_____

What sometimes keeps you frozen when it comes to fulfilling your purpose? How does knowing that God is not expecting you to be a "superstar," but just a woman who is dedicated to him, help you with your fears?

_____

_____

_____

When God Is Ready, He Will Reveal His Vision!

God gives each of us something that makes us smile in ministry, and he will surround us as needed with like-minded people to help us complete the unique purpose he has reserved for us on earth. I had searched for a long time before God more fully revealed to me my individual, long-term purpose. His clarity was not available to me one nanosecond earlier or later. I'm convinced the reason he did not make it easy on me was so that I would be passionately motivated to encourage other women who are in the midst of the long, long, long process.

_____

_____

_____

_____

_____

_____

_____

_____

_____

_____

_____

_____

> What are some specific reasons that God might be delaying the complete revelation of your purpose? How might the waiting and searching be preparing you today for what he has for you in the future?

The Sojourner's Guide to Receiving God's Vision

The following suggestions are intended to help you prepare yourself to listen for God's thoughts and receive his vision for your life.

1. Pray.

   The best thing to do while you anticipate God's revelation of a vision for your life is to pray. Pray that you will hear God and be made pliable in his hands. Pray, too, for God's perfect timing, that he will ready the hearts of the people he is sending you to serve. [You can go deeper into prayer and purpose with another book in this series, Praying for Purpose for Women.]

   Record your prayers here so that you can look back on them when the answers come and remember God's faithfulness!

   _____

   _____

   _____

   _____

   _____

   _____

   _____

   _____

   _____

   _____

   _____

2. Ask others to pray.

   Surround yourself with loving, supportive people who will pray with you regarding God's vision for your life. Ask them to pray specifically that you will be receptive to God's best for you.

3. Be confident.

   Confidence means "with faith." For this step, you need faith that will move mountains, faith that will unleash the power of God. You must believe that God will cast the vision he has always had for you!

   Talk to God in writing about nurturing your faith so his vision for your life will become apparent to you.

   _____

   _____

   _____

   _____

   _____

   _____

   _____

   _____

   _____

   _____

   _____

   _____

   _____

   _____

   _____

   _____

4. Practice patience.

   Practice waiting graciously in all of your daily activities, including standing in line at the bank or grocery store. Practice patience by engaging in activities that require it, perhaps flying a kite or planting a garden. In addition, take time to sing, play, and relax so you can learn to slow down and enjoy the journey.

5. Ask God specifically to speak to you.

   If you think you want God to speak to you, you may first want to answer two very important questions:

   Do I really want and expect God to speak to me? Am I really listening?

   _____

   _____

   _____

   _____

   _____

   _____

   _____

   _____

   _____

   _____

   _____

   _____

   _____

   _____

   _____

   _____

   _____

   _____

   _____

   _____

   _____

   _____

   _____

Personal Pathway Questions

Without analyzing your answer, quickly jot down what you think is God's vision for you.

If you are not able to answer this question right now, please don't worry about it. A wide variety of clarifying work is involved. Look back over your responses to the questions at the end of each chapter in this journal to help you determine your next action step. The intentional work you do now will invite an answer. Also, don't forget to rest in the Lord, pray, and believe that God will reveal his plan for you.

_____

_____

_____

_____

_____

_____

_____

_____

_____

_____

_____

_____

_____

_____

_____

_____

God's Wisdom for the Pathway

The "Deborah" Step of Life:
Eagerly Anticipate that the Lord God Almighty Will Reveal His Vision to You.

For a lesson from Deborah, prophetess and judge, during this step of your life, read her story in Judges 4 and the celebratory *Song of Deborah* in Judges 5. Deborah was the only known female judge of Israel, and she was characterized by her wisdom.

Jabin, the king of Canaan, and Sisera, the commander of the king's army, had terrorized Israel for twenty years. Deborah summoned Barak, her countryman, in the name of Yahweh, and informed him that God would deliver the enemy into his hands. Barak refused to go unless Deborah went with him. She did go, and the enemy was soundly defeated. Expect God to give you a clear vision, like he gave Deborah.

_____

_____

_____

_____

_____

_____

_____

_____

What are your thoughts and impressions about this story? What can you take from Deborah's story and apply to your journey toward purpose?

_____

_____

Take Courage

As we continue on the pathway to purpose, we may be tempted to laugh out loud at the sight of our next stepping-stone, *take courage*. We can't begin to imagine how we can muster the courage to tackle a God-sized life purpose. But the good news is that we don't have to muster anything. Courage is a gift from God. To receive it, we need only show up and rely upon God's complete faithfulness.

What are your thoughts about the idea that you don't have to muster up courage, but that it is a gift from God? Is this a new idea to you? How might this change your idea of being courageous as you seek your life purpose?

God's Gift of Courage

Jesus *commands* that we be fearless. Taking courage is an act we initiate that is based on something real and reliable—God's steadfastness. As we begin to grasp the truth of his presence with us, we can exhale with relief and move forward with courage. There is no reason to be afraid when Jesus is with us! He is the reason we can be fearless. Whether our fears vanish or whether we press on toward our goal even though we are afraid, we will receive courage as we obey God and experience his faithfulness.

Why do you think that Jesus commands us to be fearless? (See Matthew 14:27.) Apply this principle of taking courage to some specific fears in your life. How can the knowledge of God's presence and faithfulness give you the gift of courage in those areas?

Why Is Courage So Important?

Fear impacts your life purpose. Once fear has you in its wicked grasp, it blocks creativity, productivity, and relationships. So, when you face your fears by taking hold of God's courage, you regain your capacity for experiencing these things as you live out your life purpose.

Below are some of the more common fears that can sidetrack us from pursuing God's purposes:

- Fear of Ridicule and Criticism
- Fear of Success
- Fear of Being Found Out
- Fear of Failure

Add your own fears to this list (or journal about how those above specifically affect your life).

_____

_____

_____

_____

_____

_____

_____

_____

_____

_____

_____

_____

Here are God's tools for helping you counteract these common fears:

- Ask yourself: Do I really intend to let somebody's comments or criticism keep me from stepping out in faith to do the work God gave me to do?
- Recognize that true success is only what God views as success, not what others think or say.
- Look for evidence of God's faithfulness in your life, taking courage that you can be your true self because God is taking care of you.
- Realize that everyone fails, but God always forgives.

Ask God to reveal to you ways in which you can counteract these fears with his gift of courage.

_____

_____

_____

_____

_____

_____

_____

_____

_____

_____

_____

_____

_____

_____

_____

_____

The Sojourner's Guide to Taking Courage

The following suggestions will help you step securely on the rock of courage. Take as much time as you need to complete the steps that are most helpful to you, and repeat them as often as necessary to continue stepping forward with courage.

1. Use the Fear Hierarchy Approach.

    Make a list of all the things you fear about living out God's purposes for your life. No matter what your fears are, rank them in order from least to worst. Pray over your list, and ask others to pray on your behalf that God will reveal the truth about your fears as they relate to his purpose for you. Then, take a stand and boldly claim God's promise that he will be with you. (Joshua 1:5) Next, take a baby step and offer one of your lesser fears to God. Keep working the list, fear by fear, for as long as it takes. Reward yourself each time you overcome a fear. (No, not a shopping or food reward!)

2. Ask yourself two questions.

First, ask yourself, *How does fear keep me focused on myself?* Write down your answer and review it in a week. If it fills you with a godly sorrow, repent of your self-focus.

_____

_____

_____

_____

_____

_____

_____

_____

Second, ask yourself, *What has fear stolen from me?* Write down your answers and show them to a friend. Ask for advice on how to take courage against your fears.

_____

_____

_____

_____

_____

_____

_____

_____

_____

3. Apply the "Just-Eat-Your-Spinach" Approach

    Sometimes you just have to go ahead and eat your dreaded spinach—by giving your first speech, by presenting your idea for a novel, or by making your difficult request—before you have time to smell and taste the awful stuff called fear. Sometimes the best course of action is to just "go for it," even when you're afraid of what is ahead. Trust God to see you through.

    Try this approach with a smaller fear first and record what happens. Then try a larger fear and record that. Writing down your victories will be a courage-builder and reminder of your progress.

4. Feed Your courage with the Word of God.

   *There are plenty of courage-building passages in Scripture.
   Search for some using a concordance or Bible software. Then
   read them, meditate on them, and journal about them.*

Personal Pathway Questions

1. What are your greatest fears about your life purposes?

    _____

    _____

    _____

    _____

2. Which fears, if any, have you successfully released to the power of
    God?

    _____

    _____

    _____

    _____

3. What is God nudging you to do about one or more of your fears?

    _____

    _____

4. What is your response to this quote from pastor Adrian Rogers:
    "Don't be afraid of the will of God. The will of God will not take
    you where the power of God cannot keep you"?

    _____

    _____

    _____

    _____

    _____

God's Wisdom for the Pathway

The "Esther" Step of Life:
Take Courage.

For a lesson on courage from Queen Esther for this step of your life, read Esther 1-10. Esther was called upon to risk her life in order to save the Jewish people, and she responded by taking the risk, saying, "If I perish, I perish."

If God gave you a bold assignment today that caused you to be afraid, would you carry it to completion, no matter what? Would you, like Esther, pray and complete a spiritual fast (and ask others to do the same) before you began? Ask God to give you his power to obey him, when you can't get over your fears, so that nothing interferes with what he has in mind for you both now and later.

Bring Glory to God

One final leap, and your life becomes part of the inviting landscape you longed for from the other side of the stream. The step you are about to take is truly the most miraculous and joyous step of all: *Bring glory to God by completing the work he gave you to do.* You see, you are a *poiēma*, "God's workmanship." You are his magnificent magnum opus, a precious masterpiece of enormous love. You can offer God no greater worship than to magnify him with your entire life.

The composer Johann Sebastian Bach is widely known for adding to his musical compositions the inscription *SDG*, the Latin initials for *soli deo gloria*, which means, "to God alone be the glory."

> How about you? Do you desire to exalt God with every action you take? Are you eager to add the inscription *SDG* to your life's symphony?

How Can You Possibly Complete the Task?

Once you have caught sight of God's vision and accepted his big life purpose for you, it is perfectly normal to wonder how you are to accomplish the task. Jesus is our example of how to do what God asks of us. While he was doing his Father's work on earth, Jesus continually prayed for guidance and strength so that he could complete the huge task before him. God is the one who will provide the strength and resources.

What specific resources do you know that you need God to provide for your own life purpose? Read Matthew 4:1-11; 14:13-21; and 26:36-42. Make some notes about how Jesus sought and received resources from his Father to complete his purpose.

Discovering a Joy You Have Never Known

The best way to faithfully accomplish the work of God is by committing heart and soul to Jesus. The natural result of that intimate knowledge of Jesus is joy. Joy can be defined as colossal pleasure or intense satisfaction that fills us with gladness. True joy is not based on our circumstances. It is based on our acknowledgment of what Jesus has done for us. It is being so filled with Jesus that he pours himself out into our thoughts, attitudes, and actions. Our commitment to do the work God has assigned to us is our heartfelt response to that joy.

Do you have true joy in your life right now? What steps do you need to take to get closer to Jesus so that you can experience his gift of joy?

Pathway to Purpose *for women*

There Will Be Miracles!

No matter how long it took, or may yet take, to receive your vision from God; no matter how much work you have now that your life purpose is in view, or how ill-prepared you feel, you can trust God—the Creator of all things—to supply your every need. You can expect him to go in front of you to swing open doors that were previously bolted closed. You can expect him to carry you forward on the wings of whatever miracles are needed to complete the task. As you fulfill your purpose, you'll stand amazed at the majesty of a God who has rescued you from your tiny, limited perspective and placed you strategically in his grand production.

Have you already seen miracles as you've traveled the pathway to purpose? If so, record them so you can remember them as you continue on your journey. If not, write a prayer, asking specifically for God to do the miraculous in your journey toward his purpose.

Hang on Tight!

At this point on the pathway, I believe God expects there to be no turning back. You have made your commitment to glorify him with your life, and you are meant to keep it. So, strap in and hang on tight. You are going on the ride of your life!

_____

_____

_____

_____

_____

_____

_____

_____

_____

_____

_____

_____

_____

_____

_____

Your primary assignment as you seek to fulfill your God-given purpose is to hang on, give God the glory, and focus on the tasks he is giving you each step of the way. Journal here about one of the next assignments in your own specific life purpose.

_____

_____

The Sojourner's Guide to Bringing Glory to God

The suggestions that follow will help you bring glory to God with every step you take on your pathway to purpose!

1. Share your impressions from God.

   Step out in faith and find a "Purpose Partner," a trusted Christian adviser with whom you can share the impressions God has given you about your reasons for being. Don't go through the process alone. Give someone else the privilege of witnessing a miracle-in-the-making with you as you seek to praise the Lord with your life.

   Write some things that you would like to share. Also, write down the names of a few people you might want to ask to become your Purpose Partner. Pray over each name, asking God to guide you to the person he has chosen.

   _____

   _____

   _____

   _____

   _____

   _____

   _____

   _____

   _____

   _____

   _____

   _____

   _____

2. Clean house.

   Tell the Holy Spirit that you are ready to do some more housekeeping! Let him know that you are cleaning out the lingering cobwebs in the corners of your thought life and in your actions. Ask for his help in taking out the garbage and clutter that are limiting your contribution to God's kingdom.

   Journal about the things you still need to clean out of your life, and write a prayer asking for God's help to do so.

   _____

   _____

   _____

   _____

   _____

   _____

3. Choose joy; choose Jesus.

   Do something radical: Choose joy on a minute-by-minute basis in the midst of trials, challenges, setbacks, and even your hectic schedule. Decide to be fully devoted to Jesus, the source of highest joy.

   What are a few specific ways that you can choose joy in your everyday life?

   _____

   _____

   _____

   _____

   _____

   _____

4. Record the miracles.

   Make a list of the significant miracles that God has already performed for you. Leave room for future entries!

Remember the Miracles

_____

_____

_____

_____

_____

_____

_____

_____

_____

_____

_____

_____

_____

_____

_____

_____

_____

_____

_____

_____

_____

_____

Remember the Miracles

_____

_____

_____

_____

_____

_____

_____

_____

_____

_____

_____

_____

_____

_____

_____

_____

_____

_____

_____

_____

_____

_____